PERK UP
YOUR
PROFITS

PERK UP
·······YOUR·······
PROFITS

A Proven 4-Step System
To Stimulate Revenues
While Rewarding Your
People

MOHAMED TOHAMI

Bestselling Author & Motivational Speaker

To all leaders who want to provide an impressive impact to their organizations by creating a passion-driven culture where people feel great and at the same time maximize profits.

CONTENTS

ACKNOWLEDGMENTS

Thanks to...

... Jim Cathcart, my mentor, for his generous guidance and inspiration.

... Mike Landrum, my speaking coach, for his trust and belief in me.

... Meg Yarnall, my editor, for her friendly assistance.

... Mala Baranove, my book cover designer, for her outstanding design.

... Yahya El-Hosafy, my friend and talented photographer, for the great cover photo.

... Israa, my beautiful bride, for her support and Maleeka, my daughter, the great joy of my life.

PERK UP

······ YOUR ······

PROFITS

THE STRANGE QUESTION

In the summer of 2007, a man named Rich Barton called his old friend, Robert Hohman. Hohman was taking time off after leaving Hotwire, a company that offers discounts and cheap deals on travel packages, hotels and flights. Barton asked him a very interesting question.

"What would happen if someone found the results of a company's employee survey on the printer and posted it to the web?"

Think about that.

What would happen if someone found the results of your company's employee survey on the printer and posted it to the web?

Let me give you a brief background about these two gentlemen to understand the logic behind this question.

Barton and Hohman worked together at Microsoft for several years before moving to Expedia, a company that Rich Barton founded to transform the travel industry by offering access to information about special offers and deals on flights and hotels that were only available to travel agents and insiders. Then, Barton left and opened another company called Zillow. Zillow offered access to information about home values and real estate offers that were normally only available to insiders. Finally, the men decided to join forces and create another company called Glassdoor.

Glassdoor was born to become one of the largest job and career communities that gives prospectives a sneak peek into the company to which they are applying. So if you are looking for a new job, you can go to Glassdoor and see what people are saying about the place you think you like - from the inside. What really sets Glassdoor apart is that all the content is employee-generated. It's exactly like finding your company's employee survey on the printer and posting it to the web!

Now the question is,

"Why is the data in Glassdoor so critical to you?"

Here's why...

Because if you really want to know what drives peak performance inside your company then you must pay attention to what your employees are saying.

Based on the reviews and the comments on Glassdoor, my personal experience, and some of the job satisfaction surveys out on the web, let me give you a quick idea of what goes on inside the employee's head nowadays in the corporate world.

Most employees are sick and tired of the unfairness of the corporate culture. They are asking themselves two questions almost every day. They wake up in the morning and think:

"Am I right now dying, slowly, for something I'm not willing to die for?"

And ...

"Why am I working so hard, moving so fast, feeling so lousy?"

These two questions indicate that the majority of corporate employees these days are feeling like a cog in a machine; like they are doing work that has no real meaning or value. They feel that they are in a place in which they don't belong and they are doing work that they were not born to do.

If you don't pay attention to these emotions and thoughts, one day your best talent will either ...

leave to live, or stay to die.

They will pursue their passions somewhere else, or they will stay just for the security of the paycheck but they will be totally dead. Their mind, heart and spirit will be detached from the work they are doing.

So, your number one role as a leader in your organization is to ...

... create a culture where people feel great, and at the same time maximize profits.

I'm not saying that you must pamper your people at the expense of profits, and I'm not saying that you're going to focus on customer satisfaction and profits at the expense of your people; you need to find balance. You need to create a culture in which employees feel great and at the same time, profits go up.

That is what this book is all about.

Usually, ordinary leaders hesitate to invest in their people in order to cut costs and increase profits. This book challenges this idea. It proves that it is possible to maximize your profits by investing in creative 'PERKS' for your people.

You are going to discover the secrets to stimulating revenues while rewarding your people. You will also learn how to become a heroic leader who can PERK up profits by driving peak performance in your organization and creating a passionate and attractive culture in which people feel positive and happy, and at the same ensuring maximal profits.

Our journey consists of four parts.

First, we will analyze the best practices of the world's top employers. These are the best places to work based on the surveys done by Glassdoor.

Second, based on the top employers analysis, we will highlight the seven peak performance drivers in these organizations, and how they PERK up their profits by making their people feel great and helping them perform their best.

Third, I will share with you a proven 4-step system that you can implement in your organization to PERK up your profits and integrate these seven peak performance drivers seamlessly and smoothly in daily operations.

Fourth, you will discover the leadership style that is required to influence your organization and successfully implement that system.

When you finish reading this book, you'll be equipped with a solid system and an arsenal of effective tools that will help you PERK up your profits and be the leader you've always wanted to be.

So, let's begin...

2

THE SECRETS OF
THE WORLD'S
BEST EMPLOYERS

In this chapter, we will analyze the best practices of the world's best employers from 2010 to 2013 based on the annual surveys done by Glassdoor.

I know you may wonder, "These surveys are done on US companies and the participants are US employees, so are they relevant to my region?"

This shouldn't be a concern, because as you are going to see, the best practices within these companies are universal. We can apply them anywhere in the world and to any culture. We are focusing here not on the nationalities or the geographical locations of the companies, but on the best practices that they use.

Let's begin in 2010.

What was the company listed as the number one best place to work?

It was Southwest Airlines.

Southwest Airlines, a United States airline, was the best place to work for in 2010 based on the survey done by Glassdoor.

Let's examine what its employees had to say. When you read the comments and reviews you will notice a common theme.

"SWA treats me like a person, not a number."

They treat you like a PERSON, not a number or a machine. They care about your personal life as much as they care about your work.

You can find some comments like:

"There are lots of social events. Every week there is a deck party sponsored by a different department."

"Volunteer work is encouraged inside the organization – and volunteers can even hold meetings inside the company during work hours."

"They involve people in making changes. If there is any issue, they involve people and they list their ideas as possible solutions."

So, that was Southwest Airlines.

What about 2011?

Facebook

Facebook was the number one best place to work. Let's see what their employees had to say.

The common theme in all the comments was...

"Making a difference."

People at Facebook feel like they are making a huge impact in the world. You read comments like:

"We are making the world more open and connected."

"It's a great innovative company that's in the business of building great communities."

"There is freedom to think outside the box; in fact there is no box."

At Facebook, you're free to think of a new feature. When you implement the feature, it will impact the world the next day. That's why people feel they are connected to a higher purpose.

That was Facebook in 2011.

Moving to 2012...

The best place to work was...

Bain & Company

Bain & Company is one of the largest business consulting firms in the world. Here the common theme among what their employees had to say was...

"Unparalleled opportunity to learn and grow."

You read comments like:

"They have a network of well-connected offices around the globe and this gives me a chance for international transfer, which is a life-changing experience by itself."

"They invest a lot in world class training and mentorship programs to make sure that people learn the most."

And here is a very special comment –

"I absolutely love coming to work here. In fact, I miss the office and the people when I'm away."

How often do we hear this from an employee? "I miss the office and the people when I'm away."

It's amazing!

Because that comment was very rare and special, I would like to share with you more comments that will give you a closer look at what is happening inside Bain & Company – just to understand why their people love it so much.

"I didn't do consulting before business school. I was rather daunted by this new type of job. But the other members on my team and the other offices were so great about bringing me on board and kind of cluing me in as to what makes for a successful case. It was very easy to get up to speed quickly."

"We know how hard our job is, and that you can't do it by yourself. You're going to have to work with other people and it is okay to ask for help here. In fact you're encouraged to ask for help here."

"Bain supports you in your objectives no matter what they are. First and foremost, they set you up for success in consulting. There's an incredible training program, incredible mentorship program. Everyone around me is rooting for my success."

"When you come to work at Bain, you're going to be working on really important issues. You'll be working on the toughest problems. And I think that's important because everybody comes to work, everybody we hire, I think has something in common. They know they want to make a difference with their day, and the outcome of the work that our employees do is absolutely changing companies."

"I can honestly say that I have not had two weeks that were the same throughout my five year tenure at Bain. It's always changing, it's always different, and it's always quick and exciting."

"There's a huge focus on setting you up for success. And what that means is clearly defining what it takes to succeed in a project and what needs to get done."

"We think we have world class training, because we understand that when we hire a new employee, they don't come in and know how to be a manager and consultant, and they certainly don't know how to be a managing consultant the Bain & Company way. So we spend a lot of time and energy training them how to be a good Bain consultant."

"The people are Bain assets, and not only are they the brightest, most ambitious people I've ever met, most of my best friends are Bains. And, I'm not ashamed to say that my coworkers are my friends because these are the best people out there."

"It just feels different to work here. And it's very rewarding to see that the data actually shows that. That the employees who talk about the company say that it just feels different to work here too."

"I think Bain & Company is a great place to work, and I think it comes as no surprise it was rated the best place to work. I've had a fantastic experience over the last two years, I've gotten exposure to so many different industries which is what I was looking to do when I

joined a job at a consulting firm, and I've had a great time doing it."

"What we do is natural; it's part of who we are. I'm very thankful that our employees recognize that because they're not just employees; these are my friends, they're my colleagues, my peers and my teammates. And so, it's great we all feel that way about our company. It really is a special place."

"I think it's fantastic that we've won this award, but I don't feel differently now than I did when I didn't know that we had won an award, so I guess thanks for telling the rest of the world what we already knew!"

"Thanks for telling the world what we already knew."

Amazing!

Bain & Company leaders set their people up for success. They invest in developing and mentoring their people like no other. Moreover, they ensure that they hire bright, friendly and supportive people. It is very rare to hear a comment like ...

"I'm not ashamed to say that my coworkers are my friends because these are the best people out there."

It shows how much they care about the caliber and integrity of people on board.

And now, 2013.

The number one best place to work was...

Again, Facebook

What did employees have to say this time? There was actually another common theme in 2013:

"We are working with the smartest people in the world."

The focus was on the people. Facebook hires the smartest people in the world. So you see comments like:

"They expect you to be the best, which evokes the best inside you."

They tell you, you are the best. Since you're working on Facebook, then by default you are one of the smartest people in the world, which evokes the best inside you.

"The company lives up to its motto. Move fast, don't be afraid."

You are the best, you are smart, so move fast, implement new ideas and don't be afraid to make mistakes.

"They do everything to make you happy. They place you on projects you are excited about."

They don't force people to work on tasks or projects that drain their energy or do not interest them.

Since Facebook came twice on the top of the list, let me share with you more comments that will give you a closer look at what's going on inside Facebook this time.

"Our mission is to make the world more open and connected, and the people who work at Facebook really believe that."

"I am constantly inspired by the people I work with every day. The caliber, the talent, all concentrated in one place, brings on this infectious energy."

"I see people who are focused on one goal, committed, and will not stop for anything. The passion that they bring to the company -- and the energy -- is one of the things I love the most about working here."

"The common theme that I've always seen here the whole time is us being really focused on our mission to make the world more open and connected and to make an impact with our product. And that's something that will always be a core part of our culture and just our thumbprint as a company."

"Knowing that you can put out a feature today and that it will be in front of a billion people next week is just something that is really hard to find in any industry and something that you have to take advantage of every day."

"I feel really proud of working here and contributing to such an awesome product. I feel like Facebook sometimes is like a utopia in the best ways. The cool

thing about Facebook's sort of approach to that is they're really focused on removing stress from our daily lives. That makes it easy for me to focus on my daily work."

"Well I think the number one thing I would say about working at Facebook is the same thing that a lot of people would say – and did say, actually in the Glassdoor reviews – is the other people who work at Facebook. So I think bringing them all together and working together as a team, learning from each other and getting feedback from one another is all at the top of my list for the reasons I think it's a great place to work."

"I think there are lots of reasons that someone might come to work at Facebook. I think that the number one reason is because of the impact. So I think, people who are really smart and really good at what they do want to have a really big impact individually and want to be a part of something that's having a bigger impact in the world."

What do smart people want? They want to have a big impact in the world and this is what Facebook provides. It connects you with a higher purpose and allows you to make a difference in billions of people's lives.

The key here is to hire the smartest people and unite them around a mission that's larger than life.

I am sure you already recognized that these companies are some of the richest companies in the world. And as you saw, investing in creative 'PERKS' for their people didn't negatively impact their profits. In fact, investing in people was one of the main reasons for their extraordinary success. They are a living proof that you can stimulate revenues and perk up profits while rewarding your people.

Now, based on this quick analysis that we have made, I would like to ask you, "What do you think are the top peak performance drivers that these companies use to PERK up their profits and make their people feel great and hence perform at their peak level?

Let's discover the answer in the next chapter...

3

THE PERK SYSTEM

After sharing the previous analysis in my seminars, I usually ask the participants to share with each other what they think are the top peak performance drivers. I often receive answers like:

"Engagement and involvement of the people."

"They let them feel they are the owners and not the employees."

"You need to have a buy-in for each and every process they are doing in the company, so that the motivation comes from inside."

"Give them space to grow and to implement the new ideas they come up with."

"Give people an opportunity to be innovative and let them know it is okay to make a mistake because they can learn and move on."

"Being given the opportunity to think outside the box, and try not to create a box in the first place."

"Using people's strengths."

"Making them think they are the best."

I am sure you can come up with more great insights. So please, take a few minutes and write below what you think are the top 7 peak performance drivers.

1.

2.

3.

4.

5.

6.

7.

Please think before you continue reading.
(This page was intentionally left blank.)

Welcome back!

Let me share with you what I think are the top seven factors that drive peak performance inside any organization:

1. Passion

It's that infectious energy that you need inside the company. You need people who are excited, supportive, and enthusiastic. The moment the alarm clock rings in the morning should not be the worst moment of the day. Rather, it should be the evening, when the day is gone. If they are passionate, you will not need to worry about them dreading the alarm clock. You need that energy as much as they need it.

2. Strengths

Evoke the best inside them. Focus on their strengths. Strengthen their strengths and ignore their weaknesses. Assign them tasks that make them feel strong.

3. Purpose

Connect them to a higher purpose; make them feel they are making a difference. Inspire them by a great mission. Make them feel proud to belong to your company.

4. Care

Treat them like human beings, not machines, not numbers. Really care about their personal life and their professional development. Remove the factors that cause stress and distraction.

5. Innovation

Have no box to think inside or outside. Encourage them to try new things and dare to make mistakes. Support their ideas and allow them to work on their own projects.

6. Growth

Offer huge learning & growth opportunities in the company. Facilitate job rotation and international transfer, if possible. Invest in world-class training & mentorship programs.

7. Atmosphere

Make their environment fun to work in. Think of the comment that said, "I miss the office when I am away." This is because of the atmosphere and the people. Provide a place that is full of fun and free of stress, clutter or distractions.

In a nutshell, these seven peak performance drivers will allow you to create a culture where people feel great and at the same time maximize profits.

Now, we need to explore how you can implement these drivers in your company. You must have a system, a step by step process, which will allow you to easily, seamlessly and smoothly implement these drivers in your company's culture and daily operation.

This is the PERK system that we're going to explore in the next chapters in full details.

But first let me give you a quick overview...

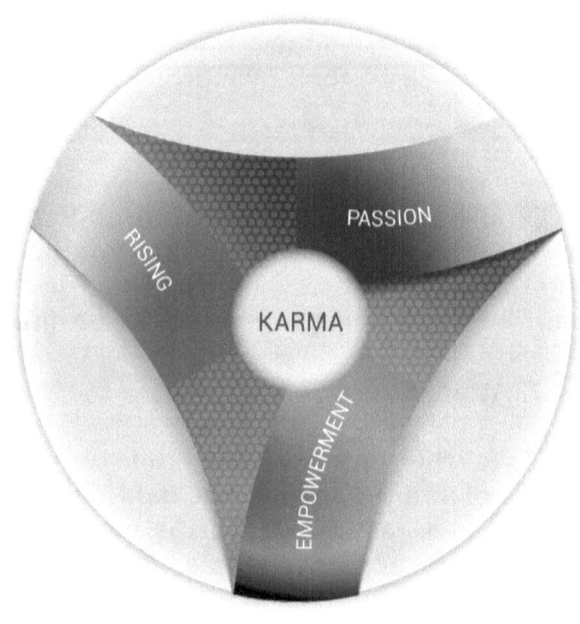

Fig. 1 – The PERK System

As you can see in figure 1, the PERK system for stimulating revenues while rewarding your people consists of four parts. Each letter in the word 'PERK' represents a specific part of the system.

1. Passion

It all starts with **Passion**. It is that infectious energy that transforms everything. Hire passionate people, and embrace or restore the passion of existing people.

2. Empowerment

When you have energy in your company, channel it to pathways that utilize people's strengths in order to evoke the best inside them. That's called **Empowerment**. Don't force them to work on tasks that will drain their energy or make them feel weak or bored.

3. Rising

And then, when they think this is everything they can learn and get from the company, provide new opportunities for growth and development. Help them **Rise** to new levels of success. This growth will feed the energy and passion more and more, and the cycle will be repeated again and again. The energy will be channeled in pathways that utilize their strengths and make them the best they can be and when they supposedly have it all, they instead find more opportunities for growth.

4. <u>Karma</u>

In the background of all that, you have a great atmosphere. Create a place that has a good **Karma**. A place with ultimate justice, positive vibes and special care for your people. Make them love the place and feel happy and stress-free working for the company.

When you implement the PERK system in your company, expect to have the happiest people and the highest profits. It is really possible.

Now, let's get into more details about each part of the PERK system and how you can implement each step.

4

PASSION
INFECTIOUS ENERGY

In the beginning of 2007, I started interviewing top success and business gurus about their secrets of success. I asked them questions like, how did you start your success quest? What were the challenges that you faced, and how did you overcome these challenges? What were the key success factors that you learned?

One of the key questions that I was always keen to ask was, "What was the transformation point in your life?"

I was curious to know what transforms an ordinary person into an extraordinary person. I thought that I would receive different answers from each person based on culture, industry they were working in, personality, and so on.

I was surprised that every time I asked that question I received the exact same answer.

The answer always came in the form of "my life was transformed the moment that I started to listen to my heart and live with passion – doing what I love, and loving what I do."

After over 150 interviews with ultra-successful people and always receiving the exact same answer, I came to the conclusion that:

Passion Is King
And only when you breathe it in, can the transformation begin.

If you want to transform your organization and provide impressive impact, then you need to bring passion in.

Now, I know you may wonder, "Passion is not everything. What about knowledge, experience, skills? You can't solely rely on people's passion."

Let me tell you a story.

In the very beginning of my professional life, I had an interview at a big IT company.

By education, I am a telecommunications engineer. My interviewer's name was Khaled. The first question he asked me was, "Tohami, tell me what do you want to do with your life?"

I said, "I want to be a motivational speaker."

"What? What does this have to do with engineering?"

"It has nothing to do with engineering. You just asked me about what I want, not what I need. What I want is to become a motivational speaker; this is my dream. But what I need to do now is get a job and make a living."

He was shocked!

He remained quiet for a minute and then he challenged me, "Can you deliver a time management course?"

I replied, "Yes, why not?"

"Okay, listen, we have a group of 14 trainees. They are young, passionate people who are having training on our campus. I will book a room for you and you go play with them. Tell them anything about time management and let's see their feedback."

I was delighted and replied, "Okay, just give me some time to prepare my material."

"Yes, sure. Take your time, and when you are ready just call me."

When I went back home I realized the big problem into which I had gotten myself.

What I failed to tell Khaled, and what I failed to tell you, is that at that moment I knew nothing about time management. And I had no idea how to train people. So, what was "time management training" supposed to be?!

But – I saw a golden opportunity to start my career in something I really love to do for the rest of my life.

So I worked on it as if my life depended upon it. Have you ever before worked on something as if your life depended on it?

I acted like a sponge, researching and absorbing everything I could get my hands on about time management, training, creating Powerpoint presentation slides, managing people in the training room, training activities ... everything from scratch.

When I had a two-day training program that I was relatively satisfied with and thought might be good, I went ahead and called Khaled to tell him that I was ready and we agreed on the training dates. I went there on time, delivered the program and I thought that the people were happy. At least that was what their faces showed.

Three days later Khaled called me. He said, "Tohami, can you come to my office now?"

I anxiously replied, "Sure, but is there anything wrong?"

"No, everything is okay, just come to my office."

I went there and was afraid that the trainee's feedback was negative and that would be the end of my dream.

I entered Khaled's office. He stood up, smiled, firmly shook my hand and asked me to have a seat. That was a totally different reaction from the first interview. He even asked me if I wanted tea or coffee!

Then he said, "Honestly, I gave you that challenge because I believed that you would fail miserably. And that would wake you up for your real calling as an engineer, but you really impressed everyone with the course. They are telling everyone around the company that they had the best course in their lives, and how it changed the way they think and act. And I called you in today to ask you if you can deliver this course to all our employees."

"Wow. Yes. I can." I was thrilled!

And the second course I delivered in my life was time management for the employees of this company. The third course was for the top management!

The Human Resources Manager, Finance Manager, Marketing Manager, and all of the other top management were sitting in front of me learning how to manage their time.

Now, if you asked me, before that incident, "How many time management books have you read?"

Zero.

"How many time management courses have you attended?"

Zero.

"How many time management courses have you delivered?"

Zero.

"How much professional experience do you have related to time management?"

Zero.

"Do you have any life experience related to time management?"

Zero!

But what I learned was that...

Passion Turns a Zero Into a Hero

Think about it. How on earth could a fresh graduate teach top managers in a big organization how they could manage their time?

It seems impossible. Logic can never ever accept that. But that is the power of passion. Passion can do miracles, and that is why you need it in your company.

If two people are applying for the same job, one is passionate with basic skills and knowledge, and one is experienced, skillful, and knowledgeable but has little passion for the type of work, then by all means hire the passionate person. Don't worry if they lack some skills or knowledge. Their learning curve will be super fast.

You cannot replace the energy that can do miracles if it is not already there. You need to bring on board people who will give it all that they have got. They will not make their primary focus their salary increase or deserved promotion. They just love what they do and are deeply satisfied. That way of work leads to miracles. Expect miracles from passionate people.

When you embrace people's passions at work, they will feel they are...

... called to work, not forced to work.

That's a BIG difference. Passionate people wake up every morning feeling that they are called to work. They love going every day to their offices. They don't feel obligated or forced to work there because they need a paycheck. You need the willing, loving spirit inside your company.

Moreover, you will automatically resolve two of the biggest corporate life problems...

1. The Work/Life Balance Myth

Age 4: He was composing music.

Age 8: He scored 1,500 out of 1,600 possible points on the SAT, the most widely used college admissions exam in the United States.

Age 9: He attended Chicago's Loyola University and was still delighted in reading children's books.

Age 12: He entered medical school.

Age 21: He completed his PhD in molecular genetics and cell biology.

Moreover, he has a black belt in tae kwon do. And he is a noted pianist.

He chose medicine because he wants to make a great contribution. He says, "We'll just have to see where life takes me, but really, I haven't done anything yet."

I'm talking about Sho Yano, a former child genius and the youngest student to receive a medical degree from the University of Chicago by age 21.

What a big, well integrated life he is living!

Probably the first question that came to your mind is how did he find time to do and maintain balance between all that?

Before we examine Sho Yano's secret to finding balance, let me ask you a question...

"How old you are now?"

Don't get me wrong.

If you take a look at your life to evaluate what you've accomplished, would you be proud of the life you've lived so far?

So many people claim that they are too busy at work that they can't find time and energy to do what they want in life.

You wish to find a secret formula to balance life and work. You wish to live a bigger life and broaden your experiences, but you are totally stressed and out of balance.

When you turn to experts for a work/life balance advice, you usually get this answer:

"You must learn how to separate work from life"

For me this is B.S.

The legendary Steve Jobs of Apple said, "Your work is going to fill a large part of your life and the only way to be truly satisfied is to do what you believe is great work. And the only way to do great work is to love what you do."

So the advice of separating work from life is not practical and is pure non-sense. If you carefully examine Sho Yano's life, you'll find the secret to balance life and work.

Here's the secret...

Sho Yano lives an integrated life

Everything he does is an integral part of his personality and lifestyle. He honors his heart's desire. Although his primary work is in the medical field, he is a highly accomplished person in other fields.

The reason behind that is that his work gives him positive energy that extends to other areas of his life. Simply, he is PASSIONATE. And when you live with passion, you live an integrated life that you don't want to separate its parts.

Think integration, not separation

When you do work you love and have a great cause to live for, your life becomes integrated. Work becomes part of your life and your life becomes part of your work. Everything you do has its role in the bigger meaning and purpose of your life.

That's real balance.

When your work energizes your life and your life energizes your work, you'll not feel that you're actually working. Everything will be an integral part in the big picture of your life.

Trying to separate work from life means that your work doesn't match with your passion and purpose in life. It doesn't represent who you truly are or what you want to be. It means that you're selling your life at work to earn a few bucks at the end of each month. And you don't even have time or energy to spend what you make on any pleasure you wish.

For many people, a balanced and happier life is associated with the dream of ...

- no longer being an employee
- no longer having your schedule dictated by others,
- no longer having your vacations taken by permission
- no longer having to obey incompetent superiors
- no longer having someone else determines your income.
- no longer having to live your life on someone else's terms.

If you want a balanced life, you must do work you LOVE! Period. There is no other way to find and maintain balance.

If you truly want to help your people live a balanced life, then embrace their passions. I'm not saying you can have 100% passionate people by tomorrow. But at least, you can start today injecting passion into your company, so that you have a passion–driven culture in the near future. The more passionate people you bring on board, the more profits you will have. If you think that making the transition to a culture of passion at this moment is an impossible mission, then you need to discover the power of starting small.

"Nothing is particularly hard if you divide it into small jobs" - Henry Ford

If you start small down the right path, then you will slowly transform your company and your people's lives into a masterpiece of joy and excellence. As the momentum builds up, you'll move faster than you could imagine possible. And always remember that...

"Slow motion is better than no motion"
- Joel Runyon

Follow Sho Yano's secret to living a balanced life. The key is to think integration, not separation. Embrace your people's passions and help them do what they love in order to become a complete, well integrated entity. Encourage your people to live their lives as a whole. Don't separate it into pieces. Otherwise, you and them will be crushed by stress and unfulfillment.

2. Time For Money: Is This a Fair Trade?

Someone asked the Dalai Lama, the spiritual leader of Tibet, what surprises him most. This was his response...

"Man, because he sacrifices his health in order to make money. Then he sacrifices money to recuperate his health. And then he is so anxious about the future that he doesn't enjoy the present; the result being that he doesn't live in the present or the future; he lives as if he is never going to die, and then he dies having never really lived."

Our behavior is very surprising indeed. For example, it's really surprising to see the vast majority of people seeking happiness by following "a day's work for a day's pay" approach to life.

How on earth can a person think that this approach brings happiness?

Truth is that it cheapens us! You were born to follow your passion and create art that makes a difference.

"The moment you're willing to sell your time for money is the moment you cease to be the artist you're capable of being." - Seth Godin

You can never ever find happiness, freedom or fulfillment in trading time for money. Let's examine better types of trades. Here are 5 better things you can exchange for money other than time.

1. Uniqueness

"A work of art is the unique result of a unique temperament" - Oscar Wilde

There is something unique about you. Find what it is and you can create work of art that takes the world by surprise.

Nick Vujicic has transformed his unique situation of having no limbs into a message that inspires millions and pushes them beyond limits.

2. Change In Status Quo

One of the best forms of art is one that causes a change in the status quo. When Apple introduced the iPhone, it changed the way we used mobile phones forever.

It didn't only change the entire mobile industry, it also changed the way we live our lives.

3. Solution To An Interesting Problem

Have you heard of the HurriQuake nail?

This is a construction nail designed by Ed Sutt to provide more structural integrity for a building against the forces of hurricanes and earthquakes. The HurriQuake was honored as the grand award winner for Best Innovation of the Year, 2006.

Instead of settling for being an ordinary civil engineer, Ed was determined to make a difference instead of following a manual.

"The nail's design began when its inventor, civil engineer Ed Sutt, traveled to the Caribbean in the wake of Hurricane Marilyn. Sutt's trip to the Caribbean was part of a team examining the wreckage of the 80% of the island's homes and business that had been destroyed in the hurricane's winds of 155 km/h. The finding among the homes that had been destroyed was that wood failure was not the cause of destruction; instead, the findings showed that the nails holding the wood together had failed, leading to the buildings' ultimate collapse."

- Clynes Tom, Popular Science

That's a perfect example of an enlightened trade used by a difference maker.

4. Something New

One of the best marketing and branding insights I've ever learned is, "You don't have to be the best, you only need to be the first"

Being a pioneer in any given field is invaluable. Apple took our minds by storm when it introduced the iPad. It was a brand new category of mobile devices that we've not seen anything like it before. They created a whole new line of business and production.

5. A Movement

Create a movement or lead a tribe against a global problem or to serve a popular cause. Examples of famous social movements are:

Civil rights movement: ensures one's ability to participate in the civil and political life of a state without discrimination or repression.

Women's liberation movement: fights for equality in society between men and women.

Slow food movement: an alternative to fast food that encourages farming of plants, seeds and livestock characteristic of the local ecosystem.

These types of trades are much better than

"time for money". YOU and your people are VERY valuable and there is a much better way to live and work rather than "a day's work for a day's pay".

When you're passionate about something, there will be much more to life than the "time for money" trade. Your passion will inspire you to create art that will change the world. Helping your people follow their passions is a surefire way to do work that matters.

The Other Side of The Coin

Loving your job is just one side of the PASSION coin. The other side is being passionate about the company's mission.

If employees don't believe in the mission of your company, if they're not passionate about and proud to work at your company, they'll leave at the first opportunity. They will go where they feel they are contributing to a bigger mission. They will still do the same job they love, but for a company that servers a greater purpose. So, you need to get the buy-in and win the hearts of your people.

Most companies tackle this issue by relying heavily on long, boring, very hard to understand (or even remember) mission and vision statements. They post it everywhere, so that people are always reminded of "our mission, our vision."

I challenge you to find an employee in your company who can remember or clearly state your mission or vision statement.

In order to win your people's hearts, I would

like to suggest a tool that's much more powerful than mission and vision statements. This tool will make your people crazy about your company and its mission.

What Is That Magical Tool?

Well, several years ago, I had a speaking coach named Mike Landrum. One day, I sent him a recording of a motivational seminar I did online so that he could give me his feedback. It was an online seminar for which people from anywhere in the world could dial-in and listen to me speaking.

I was already so happy and proud of this teleseminar because the feedback was really great. I remember a lady cried at the end of the seminar because she was so touched by the message. Another lady said that the last weekend she had attended a two-day workshop for $3,000 and yet she believed that the 60 minutes she spent listening to me were much more valuable to her than those two days and $3,000.

So, I was proud, and so was Mike. At the beginning of our coaching call he said, "You are really impressing me, making a lot of progress, and I am very happy for the feedback you got from your audience. But would you allow me to tell you the truth?"

"Yes, sure."

He said, "Tohami, you are not original."

I was really confused and shocked. I replied, "What do you mean by that?"

He said, "You didn't come up with anything

special or unique. We all know that in order to succeed in life, we must have a goal and a mission, to have a purpose, be patient, persistent, etc. There was nothing fresh and original about what you said."

I replied with slight disappointment and anger, "Yes, there is nothing new about being successful, these are universal principles. And I didn't copy any expert and what he says word by word. I just came up with my own perspective on the topic."

"I'm not accusing you of copying anyone, but what I'm saying is that you are not original."

"Ok, could you please tell me how I can become original?" I was frustrated.

"Who is your favorite motivational speaker?" he asked.

Without hesitation I replied, "Les Brown."

"What do you like the most about Les Brown?"

"I'm fascinated by his energy and the intense passion with which he tells stories. Have you seen his speech in front of 10,000 people in a stadium, when he was telling his story that ended with his signature message, "you gotta be hungry!"?

"You got it, Tohami."

"Got what?"

"That's the secret of being original."

"Sorry, I do not get it."

He said, "Tohami, world-class public speakers are world class **storytellers**."

"That's powerful Mike. I know the power of stories. But I always believe that my life has nothing special to tell or share with people. There's no drama in my life." I replied.

He said, "You don't need any drama. All you need to do is tell your audience a story that illustrates how you learned that lesson or how you applied that lesson in your life. This way they will believe you, they will connect with you and relate to you. This is how you become original. They can hear an idea from anyone. They can hear the perspective from anyone. They can hear the principle from anyone. But they can never hear the story except from you, simply because it's your story. This is how you become original and special. Tohami, people love stories. Your stories will make you memorable and different. Stories stick. Stories stick."

In order to win people's hearts inside your company, you must tell your company's story.

Great leaders are world-class storytellers. Great companies and empires are built around a signature story.

Tell your people the story of why you exist in the first place. The story will stick and will make them crazy about your company.

Steve Jobs delivered Stanford University's commencement speech in 2005. It was just fifteen minutes long and it consisted of just three stories. He even didn't perform the stories; he read them from his notes. I consider that speech one of the most inspiring keynote speeches in history. That's the power of stories.

You need to inspire your people by your story. Tell them an inspiring, well-crafted, true story that they can proudly share with their friends, outside and inside work. People don't remember or share vision or mission statements, but they always remember and share good stories. Your story will make you original and special in the minds and hearts of your employees.

Let's summarize the first part of the PERK system – **Passion**.

You need to bring passionate people in if you want to have that infectious energy in your company. And you need to help existing people to discover and follow their passions. Then, you must inspire them with your company's story that makes them crazy, proud and passionate about your company and its mission. That's the first step to creating a culture where your people feel great and at the same time maximize your profits.

Passion Is King!

5

EMPOWERMENT
NATURAL STRENGTHS

We often see employees who are passionate but find themselves drained when they are forced to work on certain tasks.

For example, they find themselves having to attend long, boring meetings, or fill in boring administrative reports that take hours to finish. They love the core of their work, but a big chunk of their time is wasted on tasks that make them feel weak. You need to make sure people utilize their strengths the best way they can.

"Many of us feel stress and get overwhelmed not because we're taking on too much, but because we're taking on too little of what really strengthens us."
- Marcus Buckingham

There are two ways to help your people leverage their strengths.

1. Weaknesses vs. Strengths

I would like to share with you a story of a man called Michel Fortin.

Michel had a very miserable childhood by all means. He was born with a minor physical disability, and he was abused by an alcoholic father who could not accept that he had "failed." To his father, Michel was regarded as a failure and treated as such.

As a result, Michel lived a secluded childhood in an attempt to avoid his father, and the rest of the world, as much as he could. He spent most of his childhood isolated in his room and spent all his time writing and expressing his emotions and feelings on paper.

When he grew up, his first job was in sales. You can imagine the contrast. It's totally against his natural ability. A sales person is supposed to be outwardly confident and powerful. But he was trying to follow advice he heard from Ralph Waldo Emerson: "Do what you fear and the death of that fear is certain."

He struggled. He spent a month at his office and had made zero calls, zero sales effort. Finally, his manager came to him and said, "Why can't you make any sales? Look, I will give you one more month with us. If you cannot achieve your targets, I'm sorry; we cannot have you working for our company."

Now, if you were in his shoes, what would

you do?

He decided not to quit. He believed that his personality wouldn't fit any other job and that he must face his fears. So, he thought, "Okay, now I have some weaknesses. Actually not some – I'm mostly full of weaknesses. There's no way I can improve my weaknesses in one month."

Therefore, he directed his thinking from the weaknesses to the strengths. When he examined the things he was already good at, he could only find one thing: writing.

He had spent his whole childhood writing his emotions and thoughts on paper.

Here is what he did with his only strength...

He got the product that he was supposed to sell. Then he got a sheet of paper, and a pen and started to write a sales letter. He listed all the features and benefits of this product and the great things that would happen to you when you use it. At the end of the letter he left a note for his prospects to contact him if they would like to see a demo or buy the product. Finally, he took the letter, put it inside an envelope, and started to send the letters to his prospects.

Now, with this creative strategy, he had an advantage over other sales people. Usually, on the phone, sales people face a lot of gatekeepers until they reach the decision-maker or the ideal client. The envelope easily passed the gatekeepers. As a result, more people got Michel's letter, started reading it, and were impressed. They had an intense desire to own that product. The writing style was so persuasive and captivating that they started calling him and ordering.

By the end of the year he became the number one sales person in the company. Number one.

And now, Michel Fortin is one of the best copywriters in the world. He once wrote a sales letter online that sold one million dollars of a certain product in 24 hours. That's how powerful his copy is.

Today, you can see a man with an unmatched self-confidence, self-esteem and remarkable success. He is totally healed. You would never recognize any weaknesses in his character now.

Why is that?

Because he focused on his strengths.

Here's what happens when you focus on your strengths...

Peter Drucker, the legendary management guru, once said, "Strengthen your strengths so that your weaknesses become irrelevant."

When you focus on the strengths of your team, you will evoke the best inside them automatically. Don't ever tell someone, "You are weak in these areas and we need to work on a development plan to improve your weaknesses and help you get the job done in a better way."

Instead, tell him or her about what they are already good at and give them training in that area to make them even stronger.

When you focus on leveraging strengths, expect nothing less than exceptional results. If you focus on improving weaknesses expect nothing more than average results. If this is their weakness, it is not their specialty, and you cannot expect remarkable things. Focus on the strengths of your people to evoke the best in them. Provide them with autonomy and discretion to work on tasks that make them feel strong.

Now, the question is what does it take to do that? What does it take to focus on your people's strengths?

It takes a little touch of creativity and willingness to be different.

When you sit with your team members to assign goals for the new year or to plan, brainstorm with them paths to reach these targets in different ways than before, in ways that directly use their strengths. They shouldn't be forced to do the job in the same old way that drains their energy.

Michel Fortin invented a totally new, creative sales method that no one dared to try before. As a result, he became the top sales person. I'm sure his company didn't mind which method he used! He achieved his targets, the customers were happy and hence his company was very happy. The "how" was not an issue.

Allow them to get their tasks done in whatever way they want. Encourage them to be creative, and give them autonomy, flexibility and freedom to think and create their own pathways to success.

Empower them to do what makes them feel strong

I know you may ask, "What if I encourage my team members and give them the flexibility to create their own pathways and still they can't perform?"

They are passionate, and you are giving them the freedom to put their strengths at work, and still they cannot perform.
What could be the problem here?

2. Acting as a Sweeper

Here comes the part of treating them like human beings. People are not machines that come with manuals and the manual tells you they should perform at this rate and if they are not performing at that rate you just throw it away or replace. It is not like that with human beings.
The secret to this performance problem is found in the story of a man named Richard Fenton. The story consists of four scenes. I'm going to tell you the four scenes and we will see how they all converge at the end.

Scene 1

At the age of eight, Richard was in love with dinosaurs, and he decided that he was going to deliver a lecture about dinosaurs in his basement. So he posted signs all around the neighborhood saying:
"Richard is delivering a lecture about dinosaurs on Wednesday at 2pm in the afternoon and a ticket is 5 cents."

He even charged for the event!

The surprising thing is that the basement was full of people. 30 people standing all around the basement listening to an eight year old boy talking about dinosaurs.

By the end of this lecture, his neighbor Mrs. Clark approached him and said, "Richard Fenton, you are quite a little professional speaker."

He didn't understand what she meant, but it resonated with him regardless. The sound of 'professional speaker' was really captivating.

He started to explore the topic and soon he fell in love with public speaking. He was so passionate about it. At school, when his classmates were submitting written reports, he was submitting oral reports, standing up and speaking. That lasted until he reached the age of 18. And like what happens with most people, we get sidetracked and we forget about our childhood passions for one reason or another.

Scene 2

Richard got a call from his father trying to convince him to come and work with him selling corporate vehicles.

His father was a sales legend. He was the kind of a salesman who could sell anything to anyone anywhere, at any time.

On the call his father said, "We have set up an office for you and it's time to join the big boys. You have a private desk and there's a phone book with some contact information of clients you need to call. Go and make some sales."

Richard decided to give it a try.

However, he found himself sitting at the desk for a couple months and was afraid to call strangers and get rejected. After a couple of months, he called his father and said "Dad, I can't make any sales. I really can't call strangers."

"Okay, come to my office," his father replied.

When he entered his father's office, his father said, "Okay, let's do some sales."

He picked up the phone and started calling one client after the other and by the end of the session he had ten orders. He handed the orders to Richard and said, "This is sales!"

At that moment, Richard firmly believed that he could never become like his father. He wondered what he could do. The problem on the other side was that his father didn't believe that he needed any training. For his father, making sales was easy.

The worst part was that Richard kept struggling for six years: trying to improve, trying to become like his father, and trying to work on his skills but without any success.

As you can see, his father gave him autonomy. Do whatever you want, I am not forcing you to follow a specific approach. Selling is easy. Still, Richard couldn't perform. He was so close to his passion of public speaking, and yet he wasn't doing well. There must be something wrong.

At the end of the 6th year, at the age of 25,

he decided that he couldn't handle it anymore. He quit and moved to California.

Scene 3

Richard moved to California, and the interesting thing was that the first job he got there was again, in sales!

This time it was in a retail store. He thought it would be different in a retail store because the customer comes to the seller. With his father he had to call strangers, and sell to them. Richard thought this setting would be easier.

When the first customer entered the store, he found himself face to face with him, and realized he needed the same sales skills. There was no difference at all. Face to face interaction was no different than phone calls. So again, he struggled and made minimum sales.

One day, while he was sitting in the store, he found Mr. Harold, his manager, coming in. He thought to himself, "Well, he is going to fire me. I am a big loser. Oh my God, if you can just help me to have one good day, I may have a chance to impress Mr. Harold and convince him to give me another chance to improve myself."

He was hoping to have a lucky day!

The first customer entered the door and Richard greeted him saying, "Hi sir, how can I help you?"

The customer said, "I need to buy an entire wardrobe of clothing."

Wow. What luck!

Richard started showing the customer all the options in the store and sold him $1,100 worth of clothing. This was in the 1980s, so one thousand dollars worth of clothing was a lot.

After he finished the sale and the customer walked out of the store, he went to Mr. Harold. He was proud to have made the biggest sale ever.

Instead of showing signs of being greatly impressed, Mr. Harold calmly asked him two very interesting questions, "Could you please tell me what this customer said no to?"

"He didn't say no to anything. He just purchased anything I showed him," Richard answered.

"Okay then, how did you know he was done shopping?" Mr. Harold asked.

Interesting question. If the customer didn't say no to anything, how could Richard have known he didn't want more?

Richard couldn't answer.

But deep inside himself, this is what happened. Richard had never spent in his life more than $1,000 on clothing. So he could never imagine that someone was willing to pay up to $2,000, $3,000, or even $5,000 on clothing. Once the customer reached Richard's mental spending limit, Richard stopped selling to him, because he was afraid to get rejected. He was afraid to hear the word "no."

Then Mr. Harold continued saying, "I watched you selling and you were not bad, but your fear of rejection and of hearing the word no is going to kill you. If you can overcome that, you can become one of the great ones."

For the first time in his life Richard heard someone telling him that he could be good and moreover he could be one of the great ones. Really?!

He was struggling for years just to become an average sales person. Here came a man whom he admired saying that he could be one of the greats, and the only thing standing between him and greatness was the word 'no'.

It's just a small two letter word. N and O.

So he decided that he was going to defeat it and he would go for NO. He said to himself, "If I got "no" more often, I would receive more "yes" as well. So if yes is the destination, no is how I will get there."

This made all the difference in his performance. As a result, he became an award winning sales person in the company, then manager of the store, and finally he became the vice president of the stores.

He pursued a very successful career until the age of 40. Then he decided to go back to his childhood passion of public speaking.

Scene 4

Richard quit his sales career and founded a speaking and training company with his partner Andrea Waltz. They co-authored several books, the most important one of them was "Go for No! If Yes is the Destination, No is How You Get There."

He spoke on stage to tens of thousands of

people every year, sharing with them his Go for No message, how to overcome their fear of rejection, and how to unleash their potential.

This huge transformation in his career and his performance happened when just one man believed in him and said that he could become one of the great ones.

This is your critical role as a leader. Your role is not to punish your people or blame them. Your critical and most important role is to act as a "sweeper."

Sweep away anything that stands between an employee and greatness. Tell him/her: you are good, but here is the problem, here is the obstacle, here is what stands between you and greatness. Let's work on overcoming that so you can become one of the great ones. You already have the potential.

If you focus on their strengths, if you give them the autonomy to work on the task that makes them feel strong, then you always monitor their performance and act as a sweeper, you will create a culture where people feel great. When people feel great, profits will be maximized because they will do their best work.

Let's summarize what we have been discussing so far. The PERK system starts with passion. Bring in passionate people with that infectious, positive energy you need inside the company, help existing people to find and follow their passion and inspire them with your original, well-crafted story that will make them crazy about your mission.

Channel this energy in ways that leverage the best in your people, empower them to do what makes them feel strong and sweep away anything that stands between them and greatness.

When they feel they've become the best they can be, it is time to provide more opportunities for growth and development. Help them rise to new levels of success.

How do you do that?

How can you always provide unlimited opportunities for growth and development in your company?

Let's see...

6

RISING
UNLIMITED GROWTH

Everyone has a desire to grow as a person. Ambitious people are always concerned with personal growth and fulfilling their potential. If you've passionate people on board, they will always be looking for new ways to rise and succeed.

If they are standing still, and if they are not learning new things or contributing to new projects, they will begin to look for other exciting opportunities outside your company to develop personally and professionally. Smart, passionate people always want to feel they are rising and making bigger impact.

There are two ways to automatically and naturally provide unlimited opportunities for growth.

1. The Stainless Guy

I once had a problem with the stainless counter of my kitchen. It collected some dirty spots and rust. I had exhausted all ways of cleaning it without success. I tried many popular cleaning products including some that were made only to clean stainless. The kitchen was very expensive and within a couple of months it rusted, so I felt very frustrated.

I called the company that I bought my kitchen from and complained about the situation. We agreed that they would send out a stainless steel cleaning and polishing specialist to fix the issue.

He was a young guy in his early thirties with a big bag of tools on his shoulder. I showed him the ugly, rusted stainless and all the cleaning products that I had used without success.

He looked at the stainless and smiled saying, "It will easily be cleaned, this is not a problem at all!"

I was surprised and told him, "But I tried so many expensive products and nothing worked."

He looked at the products and smiled again saying, "This b.s. doesn't work, of course. Rest assured I will not leave without giving you a bright, shiny, like-new kitchen."

He opened his big bag and brought out his polishing and cleaning tools.

Then he started the show!

He was cleaning the stainless as if he was bathing a baby. You can see the passion in his eyes. His passion compelled me to comment, "Oh, you seem to love what you're doing."

"Yes, I've been doing this for 15 years. Nothing satisfies me more than cleaning the stainless, making it shiny and making the customer happy."

I asked with shock, "You've been working in the stainless industry for 15 years?"

He said, "No, not exactly. I have been only specializing in finishing, cleaning and polishing the stainless for 15 years. I specialize in polishing and cleaning the stainless after its welding and production in the factory. I work on the finishing line."

"You're an expert then," I replied and he just smiled.

The stainless guy brought out two small bottles. One contained a transparent solution and the other contained a yellow solution. He then looked at me and said, "See these two bottles? These are the result of 15 years of experience and trial and error."

I wondered and asked, "Did you create these solutions?"

"Yes. It is a secret organic formula that I keep away from everyone."

Without waiting for me to comment, he immediately mixed the two solutions on a piece of cleaning cloth and started the magic!

I was shocked! This solution worked. It removed all the rust and dirty spots without any effort.

He told me, "This formula is very safe and made of natural materials. It doesn't include any chemicals. With a small drop I can clean all the stainless in kitchen."

I stood watching him in awe and when he finished my mind was blown away.

I couldn't resist asking him, "Have you ever thought of telling the top management in your company about this solution, so that you get a promotion, a salary raise or something?"

He replied with fear in his eyes, "Of course not. If I do that, they will give all the credit to my boss or my boss will hate me because I outdid him."

"Ok, what about contacting other companies that produce cleaning products and selling them your secret formula for millions of dollars?" I asked.

"Oh no, I never thought about that. I don't know how to reach these companies. And even if I did, they might deceive me and steal my secret without giving me anything back."

I replied with frustration, "Forget about all that, have you thought of opening your own company and producing, packaging and selling this amazing solution? You can become rich in no time!"

He aggressively replied, "Oh no, that requires a lot of legal papers, approvals and taxes. I'm not into this headache at all. Look sir, save what you're trying to say. I'm happy like this. I focus on being a specialist at what I am doing and making the customer happy. That's all I want."

I gave him some really good tips. But I stayed up all night thinking about this stainless guy.

How many employees do we have in our companies that are in the exact same situation as this stainless guy? How many times do we see people who have different treasures inside them, but they are afraid to share?

They are under the perception that no one would listen, and if someone listened, it would be a long, complicated process to implement their innovative idea.

You MUST always encourage innovation like no other. Encourage your people to share their hidden treasures. If you give them room for innovation, thinking outside the box, and working on their own creations, you will create unlimited opportunities for growth.

When they think they reached the saturation, and think there's nothing more to learn, they will recall that they are free to think of a new idea, and they will have all the support from the company to implement that idea.

If you have a lot "stainless guys" in your company, this is a big loss. Create a culture where people are encouraged to create and innovate. There's no box for thinking and innovation.

2. The Secret of World-Class Training

The second thing you can offer your people for unlimited opportunities for growth and development is world class training. But there is a twist.

Here's how training is done in most companies...

Usually, you create a training plan that looks like this:

1. Identify competencies that need to be developed.
2. Select training providers.
3. Evaluate training programs.
4. Set a schedule.
5. Share the schedule with the managers.
6. Managers assign selected team members to go to the training.
7. People go have some fun outside the workplace.

And that's it. TOTAL WASTE!

Starting today, you need to shift your thinking from training plans to *training campaigns*. There's a big difference. The training campaign consists of three parts.

1. Marketing

You need to market your training plan as if your employees are going to pay for it from their salaries.

Oftentimes we see people going to training programs just to spend time off from work, enjoy some fun activities, and be away from their desk. That is because they don't understand the value of training. They don't know the benefits. You must explain what is in it for them and how this will boost their personal and professional skills. They must understand the high value, so that even if you ask them to pay for it from their salaries, they will agree.

Tell them, here is what we have for your growth and development; this is how you can improve your entire career or future, and really convince them.

You want them to go because they really want to learn something. They should want to go there so they can rise to new levels of excellence.

2. Experts

Please, avoid facilitators by all means. Give your employees world class education from EXPERTS.

Yes, experts are expensive. Facilitators are cheap. But think of the value that you are going to get from an expert who has been there, who is living what he's teaching. There's a difference. You get what you pay for!

It's not about someone who has good presentation skills and that's it. Focus on experts who can give them world class education like what we saw in the Bain & Company example. Experts add real life application to theories. They show people how to apply what they learn in their specific situations. They can teach with their stories and experience.

3. Coaching

When employees receive this world class education, something very important must happen. They must believe they can apply what they learned.

For example, an employee goes to a stress management course, and he gets amazing tips from the expert. But, from inside, he is 100% sure that when he goes back to work, he will still have a manager who overloads him with tasks and work, and he will find a company that never cares about his work-life balance or his personal life. He can't see how to actually implement the skills he is learning. That's a total waste of time, money, and effort.

All managers must agree to let their teams know that they should come back with an action plan that they would like to implement in the company. Team members must know that management is open to using the skills taught in training and incorporating them into daily company life. Your role as the manager is to coach them in applying the skills, and promise them that you will help them with what they will learn in the training program.

You can even ask the expert to provide follow up sessions to coach people on what they have learned and to check in.

The coaching and follow up is very important. The end of the training session should not be the end of the training. Training should be a continuous process of coaching and follow up with your people.

These three steps form a fully integrated campaign. Start with marketing so that employees are warmed up and eager to learn. Then, deliver world class education from experts who can make a real difference. Finally, coach them through a clear action plan and give them a firm promise to help them apply what they learned. Carry out that promise. This is how you maximize the training's return on investment.

However, there is a very popular dilemma in training.

"What if I invest in them, and they leave?"

My mentor, Jim Cathcart, the world's top award-winning professional speaker, author of sixteen books, expert in sales and marketing and customer service, once answered this question in a brilliant way.

He said, "Okay, you wonder what if you invested in them and they left? This is not the question. The right question is:

"What if I do not invest in them and they stay?"

The loss would be much greater.

If you have a peak performance system like the PERK system that we are sharing now, Passion, Empowerment, Rising, and Karma (great atmosphere) in the background, then the retention rate will be high.

Don't worry about them leaving. Even if they left, they will know that you are much better than other companies, and they may come back one day. Or, at least they will be good ambassadors and speak highly of you.

Invest in them and do not be afraid that they will leave. If you do not invest in them, and they stay, without passion and learning, the loss will be much greater.

If you apply these two strategies for providing endless growth opportunities, if you always encourage your people to share their hidden treasures and create a culture of open access to decision makers, if you provide them with world class training, they will be eager for it and they will know that they are in a place of unlimited opportunities for rising, growing and developing.

As a result, you will create a culture where people feel great and at the same time maximize profits.

Now, let's move on to the final step that integrates all the previous steps...

7

KARMA
ATTRACTIVE ATMOSPHERE

Have you ever entered a place and said, "This place has a really good karma"? A place with a good karma offers ultimate justice, positive vibes and special care for the people inside.

I would like to share with you an example of how to create a great atmosphere that is going to blow out your mind.

It's not about Google, or Facebook, or another giant company. It's about a privately held software firm named SAS. It's not known for offering the highest salaries in its field and they don't have stock options. Yet they were rated as the 2010 World's Best Employer by Fortune magazine.

Why? How?

If there is a heaven on earth for the workplace, it is at SAS. They have a design for living, and working, the good life. It all started 26 years ago, with **free M&M's every Wednesday**.

The free M&Ms and free Monday morning fresh fruit has grown in to state-of-the-art work out facilities, pool, and fitness classes, a health clinic, car repair, sports leagues, daycare programs, and full time artists-in-residence, among other perks. Every week, several dozen of the employees get massages at the on-site 66,000-square-foot recreation and fitness center. There's classic massage, Swedish massage, and orthopedic massage -- all designed to make workers "more aware of their bodies, move with greater ease and freedom," and "have increased energy, reduced feelings of pain, and feelings of relaxation and well-being." In fact when Google, a SAS customer, was putting together its own campus freebies some years ago, it used SAS as a model!

CEO and founder Jim Goodnight says, "My chief assets drive out the gate every day. My job is to make sure they come back." Goodnight says the "wonder" isn't that his company is so generous, but why other presumably rational corporations are not.

The idea here is simple: remove as many burdens as possible from an employee's life so that they can be as productive as possible.

When employees do not have to worry about going to a doctor's appointment mid-day because it is five minutes from their desk, or worry about what they're going to do with their kid all day during the summer, they can be much more creative and happy because there is less for them to juggle and less to think and worry about. Jim Goodnight knows that if he treats his employees well, they'll want to return. His employees are an investment, they're assets – and in order to keep the company going, he must invest in them.

Instead of stressing the employees with loads of work, Goodnight instills a 35-hour work week – five hours less than the average company – and doesn't track vacation days. People feel free to work on their own schedule whether they are night owls or more productive with scheduled seven hour days.

The atmosphere of laid-back convenience fosters relaxation. When people are relaxed, they can think more clearly, and thus their work can be more creative and more productive.

Not only that, but the efforts SAS makes on behalf of employees reminds those employees of one thing: **SAS cares**.

They care about each employee enough to make sure that they have everything they need at their fingertips. When the employees feel cared for, they will care about the company, and will give back to the company with their energy and work. There is a relationship being nurtured.

When an employee was asked about leaving SAS, he replied, "I just can't imagine leaving SAS, and I've felt that way for a very long time.

If somebody offered to double my salary I wouldn't even think about it."

SAS's low turnover rate is evidence that the employees are content; its profits and work are proof that the employees are working hard and are plenty productive. For 33 straight years, SAS's revenues have gone up -- reaching $2.3 billion in 2009, nearly doubling in seven years. SAS has never had a losing year and never laid off a single employee.

> *"My chief assets drive out every day, my job is to make sure they come back." - Jim Goodnight*

I would like to add just one word to that statement.

"Happily"

"Make sure they *happily* come back."

To feel they are called to work, not forced to work.

Let me ask you this...

... if you were working in a similar atmosphere, with such a great karma, what would be the result?

Or, in other words, why does SAS provide their people with such an exceptional atmosphere?

For several reasons:

- To help employees work from their heart, so they will give energy regardless of the income or the return.

- To help them be productive.

- To encourage loyalty.

- As Jim Goodnight said, "If you make your employees happy, they make your clients happy and thus maximize your profits."

- To show your employees you care about them and their happiness. This will make the employees care about the company in return, and thus care about its profits.

- To engage with employees, which will help them always go the extra mile since the company goes the extra mile for its people.

- To help ensure that employees are brand ambassadors outside of work. When a company is happy on the inside, it will also appear happy to the outside world – one of the ways this happens is through employees.

- The employees will believe in, and trust, the values of the company.

- If you keep employees happy, they produce more because they are not burdened with distractions.

When academicians analyzed the SAS model, they found that what SAS does leads to three key results:

1. Boost in Creativity

Imagine working in an environment like SAS. What would hinder your creativity?

In any job, you need to have some sort of maximized creativity in order to understand how you work best and to be innovative. This is especially true at a software company.

2. Reduced Distraction

If you don't have to worry about taking care of your aging parents, or day care for your children, or when to get your car repaired or go to the doctor, then you won't be distracted by any of these things when you sit down to work. You will be more productive and more relaxed.

3. Intense Loyalty

In an interview a SAS employee once said, "If someone offered me double my salary, I wouldn't leave." This is intense loyalty.

I would like to remind you that this heaven-like atmosphere didn't just appear out of thin air. It started with free M&M's on Wednesdays. That was it. Goodnight planted that seed and it grew to become an exceptional atmosphere.

So what's your M&M candy for your people?

What is the seed that you are going to plant so that it will grow in the future to become such an exceptional atmosphere?

When you provide your people with such a great atmosphere and good karma, you create a culture where people feel great and that will naturally maximize profits.

SAS has never had a losing year, or laid off an employee, even in the years of economic crisis. We are talking real profits here. Goodnight is not pampering his people and losing money. In fact, his simple approach has made him the wealthiest man in North Carolina!

All it takes is to dare to be exceptional. Don't be like other companies or leaders that always say they are different. Dare to actually be different.

What type of leaders do you need to be in order to have the power and influence to implement this system?

Let's see...

8

HEROIC LEADERSHIP

I couldn't believe my eyes when my 2-year old daughter grabbed the iPad from my hands, flicked through it until she found her favorite game, started playing and when she was done, she switched off the iPad and handed it back to me!

The question is, "What is the relation between this and leadership?"

I believe that it is not fair to consider someone like Steve Jobs a leader. He is a hero!

He didn't just influence his organization. He influenced entire generations (including my 2-year old daughter) and envisioned products that revolutionized our lives.

In my opinion...

**leaders influence organizations.
But heroes influence generations.**

The economic challenges nowadays require leaders who are courageous, different and crazy enough to pursue new pathways that can revolutionize the way we are working and living our lives. We are in deep need for more heroic leaders like Steve Jobs.

There are four main traits that you must develop in order to qualify for heroic leadership.

1. Finding Direction In The Darkness

Heroic leaders can find direction and guide people in the toughest moments.

One day, my friend Hossam and I decided to organize and deliver a training program together. The program would be a "bootcamp" and take place outside of Cairo.

We chose a location in the Baharya Oasis in the west of Egypt. A group of eighteen people joined us, most of them university students.

Part of the program was camping for one night in the White Desert, midway between Baharya Oasis and Siwa Oasis.

It was January, and before we moved on to the White Desert on the camping day, the Bedouin tour guides warned us to take heavy clothes because the weather was extremely cold at night. After about an hour on the road in our four 4x4 safari cars, we finally reached the camp location around sunset.

As this was my first visit to the White Desert, I was pleased to be greeted by beautiful weather and breathtaking nature. White rocks cover most of the sand area, resulting in an expanse of sparkling white ground. It was amazing. The weather was warm and the breeze was refreshing. We couldn't figure out why they had warned us about the weather!

As we were enjoying the magic of nature, one of the tour guides said, "Hey, guys, while we set up the camp, you can go straight in that direction to see the "Tree and Chicken" stone formation. But don't stay too long, and be sure to come back before the sun totally disappears."

We walked in the direction he had pointed to, and just a few meters later, we saw the amazing stone formation. As the name suggests, one stone was in the shape of a tree and, right beside it, was another in the shape of a chicken.

We took some photos and were enjoying our time there very much. But suddenly someone shouted, "Look over there! What is that thing coming up at the horizon?"

I looked and saw a dark red light extending across the horizon and rising up slowly. I replied with a smile, "Oh, don't worry, that's just the beautiful color of the sun reflecting on the rocks before it disappears."

"No... no... that is a sandstorm!" he shouted anxiously.

The group started to panic, everyone confirming the interpretation of that thing coming toward us from the horizon.

"It's a sandstorm! It's a sandstorm!"

We quickly formed a close group. I took the lead and started rushing everyone back to the camp.

But it was too late. Suddenly, we were in the midst of that fierce sandstorm. We could barely open our eyes. It was hard to breathe, and we could barely see our feet. The sun disappeared and the night quickly took over, leaving us unable to see our way back.

We all turned on our mobiles to use as flashlights to light the way, while the sandstorm kept on hitting us without mercy. We increased our speed, hoping to reach the camp as soon as possible.

Then someone asked me, "Tohami, are you sure you're moving in the right direction? It didn't take us that long to get from the camp to the stone formations."

"Well, I just turned my back to the stones and moved in a straight line," I replied hesitantly.

With a touch of sarcasm, he said, "Tohami, the stones are in the middle of the desert. You can turn your back to any point and move! The question is, did you turn your back facing the right direction?"

I realized the big mistake I had made, and I had no answer.

Then I said, "Hey, guys, I think we are lost!"

Everyone started to shout and panic.

"What are we going to do?"

"We're going to die!"

"Let's take that direction – I noticed this stone on our way to the stone formations."

"No, no, let's take that direction. I'm sure."

In the middle of that chaotic and scary moment, my friend Hossam luckily found a signal on his mobile, so he quickly called one of the tour guides. "Hey, please save us! We're lost."

The tour guide anxiously replied, "Why didn't you come back when you saw the storm? Didn't we warn you not to be late? Where are you now?"

Hossam couldn't believe the question! He nervously replied, "How can I tell you where we are now? We are in the desert in the middle of nowhere!"

"Okay, okay. Can you go back to the stone formations?"

"Okay, we'll try," said Hossam.

"How are we going to get back to the stones? We can't see anything," someone asked. We couldn't see beyond our feet and the sandstorm was still hitting us relentlessly.

Embarrassed, I said to myself, "Turning our backs to something and moving in a straight line is not going to work again. So just stay quiet."

We moved back hoping that we could reach the stones without deviating too much from the right direction.

And then we saw two tour guides on top of a big stone, waving for us. We rushed to them, giving them both hugs of relief.

"Thank God! You saved our lives! **You are our heroes, you are our heroes!**" everyone cheered.

When the guides pointed out where the stone formations were, we saw immediately that we had been moving in the wrong direction. In the desert, it is not enough to move in a straight line, because any slight change in direction will lead to a completely different place.

We headed back to the camp.

When we finally reached the camp, we were extremely exhausted. We just fell on the sand, thanking God that we were back safe. Everyone grabbed a bottle of water that was supposed to be used for drinking and used it to wash our eyes. They were full of dust and sand, and it was so painful that we could only open our eyes into tiny slits.

I've watched movies in which people get lost in the desert, and I always laughed at the exaggerated reactions of the actors. But that day, I realized just how scary it is to get lost in the desert. And we didn't just get lost – we got lost at night and in the middle of a sandstorm! So it was ten times tougher. We were closer to death than to life. In that situation, it was difficult to find a way to survive.

After that experience, I thought to myself, "Aren't we supposed to be the camp leaders? How come the moment we lost direction, we lost authority and the tour guides became heroes?!"

That's what happens in real life.

Normal leaders can guide people in the daylight, when everything is clear and normal. But once the way starts to get tough, dark and no body can see the light, only heroes can stand up and take the lead.

Leaders find direction in the daylight. Heroes find direction in the dark night.

When you face a challenge or a problem, like a sandstorm, and you don't know your direction, it can break you down very easily – because there's no weaker position than being without direction. It becomes nearly impossible to survive the challenge.

But the guides were the masters of the desert. They knew directions and the field better than anyone. Their knowledge and experience surpassed ours. So they just had to re-evaluate their path and identify where they needed to go to reach their destination. And that's how they led us back safely.

To become a heroic leader, you must know about your field more than anyone else. Only then you will be able to find direction in the dark night.

As a practical tip, I highly recommend that you read at least one book a month in your field or related fields. Do anything you can to expand your knowledge and experience far beyond average leaders.

2. Reshape Reality

Heroic leaders don't accept reality as it is. They reshape it.

A reporter once asked an old couple, "How did you manage to stay together for 65 years?"

The woman replied, "We were born in a time when if something was broken we would FIX it, not throw it away..."

It seems that nowadays we don't have that 'Fix' mentality at all. That's why we have problems in many aspects of our lives like relationships, work, health, etc.

In addition, our problems affect our dreams and aspirations. If we find something wrong or think that it's going to be hard to turn our dreams into reality, we throw our dreams away, instead of fixing what we see wrong as much as we can.

We easily throw away and give up on anything that has a defect, while elders always tried to 'fix' it first.

You dream about the great things you want to do in life to find yourself quickly falling back to reality and say, "But this is just a dream" And then you throw it away. Usually, you don't question reality or spend enough time trying to fix what you see wrong with it.

Here are 7 reasons why you can reshape your reality and have faith in your dream...

1. Illusion

> *"Reality is merely an illusion,*
> *albeit a very persistent one."*
> *- Albert Einstein*

How many times do you see people who have done what you thought is impossible?

Everyday we see real life examples of people who achieve the impossible. This means that reality is just an illusion.

Everything is possible. I always say, "Where there is a heart, there is a way." If you're passionate enough, you will find a way.

2. Interpretations

> *"There are no facts, only interpretations."*
> *- Friedrich Nietzsche*

Reality is what you make it. Is the color of the sky really blue?! Reality is all about interpretations.

3. Social Agreement

> *"What we call reality is an agreement that people*
> *have arrived at to make life more livable."*
> *- Louise Nevelson*

Since you didn't participate in making these social agreements that define reality, therefore you can make your own definition and take a stand as long as you're not hurting anyone.

Have you heard of this advice before, "First break all the rules"?

It is the title of one of Marcus Buckingham's bestselling books. The book appeared on the New York Times bestseller list for 93 weeks!

You don't have to comply with others' definitions of reality. You can live your life on your own terms.

> *"There is a fine line between dreams and reality,*
> *it's up to you to draw it."*
> *- B. Quilliam*

It's up to you to draw it.

4. Question

> *"Question reality, especially if it contradicts the*
> *evidence of your hopes and dreams."*
> *- Robert Brault*

Always question your reality. Ask yourself, "Is it really true? Can there be another way to interpret the situation? What would happen if I acted as if it is not true?"

Don't take everything for granted. Reality is just an illusion. That's why with a couple of questions you can turn reality upside down.

5. Sprinkle

> *"Reality is too much to take in heapfuls, but sprinkle*
> *it sparingly upon life's path and most can tread it*
> *lightly." - Terri Guillemets*

This quote triggered a very interesting question in my mind:

"Will reality remain like that all the time?"

Isn't it possible that my interpretation to reality changes over time? Isn't it possible that the things that define reality now change over time?

If you agree that what is real now will not be real in the future, then the most wise decision you should make is to take action despite of your fears of what reality holds for you.

Sprinkle reality over time and it will have minimal impact on your progress. Take action towards your dream and be prepared for the time when reality changes.

6. The Absurd

"Only those who attempt the absurd will achieve the impossible."
- M.C. Escher

Could anyone imagine that Thomas Edison could develop a form of electric lighting that was practical for home use?

Edison failed 999 times before he could make it. Despite of his cheer volume of attempts, he didn't give up. He kept on doing his absurd experiments, until he achieved the impossible.

Be happy when people call you crazy, because that's the label of difference makers.

7. Imagination

"Everything you can imagine is real."
- Pablo Picasso

"If you think you can do a thing or
think you can't do a thing, you're right."
- Henry Ford

If you can imagine that it's possible, then the world will follow your imagination. Edison saw it vividly in his mind and heart, and he imagined that it was possible. We are all grateful for his patience and perseverance.

Imagination is the most powerful tool to define reality in a way that serves your passion and aspirations. If you can imagine it, you can do it.

Don't let reality stop you from living a life you can be proud of. Don't let reality make your life's story boring to death. Don't let reality tell you that you can't apply the PERK system in your company.

Follow your passion, be courageous and make your life a story that's worth telling.

3. Cultivate Empowering Beliefs

Heroic leaders have empowering beliefs towards their pursuits.

Beliefs are acquired through our life experiences. Over the years we develop empowering beliefs and limiting beliefs. Our success in life is determined by whichever is dominant. Those with dominant empowering beliefs achieve more, suffer less and make a significant contribution, while those with dominant limiting beliefs achieve less, suffer more and do nothing of much significance.

The transformational moments in our lives happen when we switch from a dominant limiting belief to a dominant empowering belief. If you think back of an AHA moment that you've experienced, you will realize that it was a moment when you broke free from one or some of your limiting beliefs. Your newly acquired freedom creates a transformational impact on your life.

I would like to share with you a few practical ways to help you experience more AHA moments and cultivate more empowering beliefs. The more empowering beliefs you have, the more you'll enjoy your life and accelerate your success.

Here are seven great ways to cultivate empowering beliefs:

1. Read Empowering Books

Nothing contributed more to my success in life than reading empowering motivational books. I'm a prolific reader and the more empowering ideas I feed into my mind, the more confident I become and the more freedom I experience.

As the saying goes, "Garbage in, Garbage out". What you feed into your mind is reflected back on your life. Acquiring new empowering ideas about life and success will help you form new empowering beliefs. Each new book will challenge your limiting beliefs and give you real life examples of people who changed their limiting beliefs and how you too can change yours.

When I experienced some pitfalls and failures throughout my career, nothing helped me bounce back more than the empowering ideas that I was feeding into mind.

I think it was December 2007 when I was speaking on the phone with a successful entrepreneur named Amr. I congratulated him on his outstanding training business, and he asked me about what I was doing with my life.

At that time, I was growing my own side business as a motivational speaker and trainer, so I told Amr about my work delivering training programs, writing articles and ebooks for my website, and interviewing successful people about their success stories. And I also mentioned that I was working on specializing in motivational keynote speaking.

Amr was glad to know that I was still on track, especially since he had been the first person to believe in me and give me a chance to speak for his charitable organization. He had seen a special gift in me and had offered me a rare and important opportunity to deliver a series of training programs to several different audiences that ranged from a few dozen to hundreds of people.

Amr is an smart salesman and opportunity hunter. Once he knew that I was still doing training and speaking, he told me that he had another great opportunity for me.

He said, with his natural enthusiasm, "Listen

Tohami, I have a deal with a big company in the telecommunications sector to deliver a full-day training program on team building. The program agenda is already full, but I will try to call the event organizer and see if we can add a 30- to 45-minute motivational speech to the agenda."

I was so excited, so of course I jumped at the chance. "Sure, I'm more than ready!"

True to his word, Amr called me the very next day to let me know that, although it had been difficult to convince the company because they didn't know me, he had finally managed to add me to the agenda.

"Please don't let me down, Tohami," he said. "I know you're good, but I want to make sure you deliver your best. The company accepted the idea because they trust me – and I told them that I'm bringing one of the very best motivators out there!"

With great appreciation I replied, "Amr, I really appreciate your trust – and rest assured that I'll never let you down. I'm going to deliver a proven speech that I received very positive feedback on from other audiences."

As the day approached, I spent my time preparing my speech and going over every detail until it was perfect. I was ready!

On the big day, I got up early, went over my speech again, put on my best suit, and started to head out the door so I could arrive one hour before my scheduled time – but then the phone rang. It was one of Amr's team calling to tell me that the weather was AWFUL!

You see, the event was being held in the beautiful Al-Azhar Park, the largest park in Cairo with tons of gardens, open space, and a breathtaking view over old Cairo – the perfect place for a team-building event.

I looked out the window and saw that the sunny morning had, indeed, turned into a blustery and FREEZING COLD afternoon! I turned my attention back to the woman on the phone.

"Mr. Tohami, we finished our program one hour earlier due to the bad weather. Although it is absolutely freezing here, we've been trying to keep the audience until your speech – but they are complaining and saying they can't stay any longer because they are freezing. If you could come RIGHT NOW, that would be great."

"Oh! Er...well, I'm on my way then," I said

And that was one of the worst decisions I've ever made.

Given the bad weather, I should have just asked her to cancel my speech. After all, an uncomfortable – and frozen — audience would never be able to focus on what I was saying to them!

But I remembered my promise to Amr, and I didn't want to let him down. And I also thought my presentation might be light and warm enough to draw the audience in despite the terrible conditions.

So I hurried up there, and even before stepping on the stage...I was FREEZING too!

I never imagined that it would be THAT cold. I felt terrible for the audience – a hundred people frozen to their chairs, probably hoping I'd give the shortest speech in history.

Despite their discomfort, the people warmly welcomed me upon my introduction – but after that, it was all downhill. What I had feared came true...after only a few minutes, I lost the audience's attention completely. I even heard a couple of complaints.

But the worst was still to come. One of the audience members – a man in his late thirties with a white mustache, one of those people who think they know everything about everything – kept interrupting me and challenging some of the ideas I was presenting. In an attempt not to lose the rest of the audience, I had to ask him to hold his questions until the end, and invited him to an open discussion after the speech.

Instead of quieting down, he started to moan and groan and criticize, saying I wasn't listening to him. The man almost ruined my speech, and distracted the other people sitting around him.

The situation was getting out of control. At that point, I figured I should just cut my losses and hurry along to my closing. And that's what I did, with that man complaining, laughing, and criticizing until my last word.

Surprisingly, after the speech, I found myself surrounded by some enthusiastic audience members who had somehow managed to pay attention. They expressed their appreciation for a great speech.

Nevertheless, I went back home regretting

that I hadn't canceled my appearance. That's when I learned that the speaking environment is as important as the message itself. I had always ignored this fact – I thought that if my content was attractive enough, I could overcome any environmental condition. I was wrong!

Anyway, the next day I received the evaluation from Amr: only 25% of the people considered the speech "excellent." My guess is that those were the people in the front row or those who were wearing enough clothes to keep warm, which meant they were actually able to listen to my speech!

On the other side, one of the comments said that the event was more than perfect...

..."except for Tohami's speech, which was the worst part of the day."

I think I can guess who said that!

In fact, I read that evaluation and SMILED!

Even I was surprised by my reaction. I SMILED at a situation that most speakers would consider a BIG failure.

But I couldn't stop smiling! And you know why? Because that experience had been the biggest – and only – failure in my speaking career...which for me meant that a big success was just around the corner!

I'd read enough motivational books and success stories to know that every success lies on the other side of failure. If I didn't know that failure always precedes success, I would have totally broken down and given up on my passion and my dream.

What happened to me that day could make

just about anyone decide to never step foot onstage or speak in public again – at least, those who aren't prepared and passionate about what they are doing, or who don't know anything about the art and science of success and failure.

And if hadn't had that knowledge to hang on to, I might have caved too.

Experiences like these illustrate just why it is so important to fill up your mind and heart with stories of success and words of wisdom – positive gems to hang on to when times get tough. Like Zig Ziglar said, "Motivation is like a shower — you need it every day."

If you have a burning desire in your heart to create, experience, or be something special, hold tightly to it, hug it close when the world outside gets cold and scary.

And when you fail, just SMILE.

Face your failure with a SMILE on your Face.

Why? Because you know in your heart that success is waiting for you just around the corner! Success is the next logical step. Learn the lesson from your failure, and move forward looking for the success that is waiting for you.

I learned my lesson that day, and then spent the next three years working on mastering the science and art of keynote speaking. I found a great speaking coach named Mike Landrum, joined the Cairo Toastmasters, and even became president of the association two years later, which gave me the opportunity to deliver lots of successful speeches.

One of my most successful speeches was a

15-minute keynote speech about the new trends in training and development in 2010. The event was held in a big annual training conference for an audience of over one hundred HR and training managers in the telecommunications industry. My presentation was highly acclaimed and considered the best presentation in the whole event, although it was preceded by great PhD speakers and training consultants with 20+ years of experience. But the passion and uniqueness with which I delivered my speech left a lasting impact on the audience. And a few years later, I shared the stage with Amr at a big leadership conference in Qatar!

For you, hang on to your daily motivation and study the stories of successful people, which will give you the inspiration and encouragement you need in your moments of failure.

You know that failure is inevitable – just be prepared for it, learn your lessons from it, work on yourself and sharpen your skills, and get ready for your next mega-hit.

2. Question your Beliefs

Sometimes we own wrong beliefs which are actually not true. We just formed them in after a certain life experience, but this doesn't mean that they are necessarily true or at least not true ALL the time.

When you question your beliefs, you assume that they might be wrong or that they are not helping you anymore to achieve what you want. And that is the first step to break free from your limiting beliefs.

Question your beliefs and face your life as it is now or as it is likely to unfold.

3. Keep an Eye on Inspiring Success Stories

When you read stories of people who overcame adversity and rose up from the trenches to fulfill big dreams, you feel empowered to follow the same path.

Success stories give hope and help you recognize the beliefs the lead to failure and the beliefs that lead to success. This way you can clearly see the type of beliefs you need to cultivate to live a notable story.

Make it a habit to always be searching for new inspiring success stories to empower you to live your own success story.

4. Connecting With Empowering People

Surrounding yourself with passionate, successful and empowering people forms the greatest support system you can have to achieve all your goals.

Empowering people can motivate you, encourage you or lift you up when things go wrong or tough. They can hold you accountable and help you stay on track. It doesn't make sense to hang out with negative people who hold disempowering beliefs about life. This won't do you any favor.

Networking with important people, those who have made it to where you want to go, is the best thing you can do to skyrocket your passion. Connecting with your mentors or role models is probably the most powerful source to find and cultivate empowering beliefs.

Those people are guaranteed to help you replace any limiting belief you might have with an empowering one. For example, what gave my speaking career a boost was a very simple advice from my mentor and executive speakers' coach, Mike Landrum.

I always read about the importance of storytelling in public speaking, but I always had the belief that nothing about my life was special or worth sharing on the stage. That until Mike challenged this belief and helped me mine the treasures in my life. As a result, my speaking skills jumped up to a whole new level -- the level of PROFESSIONAL speakers.

5. Simplify

Simple living is a secret uncommon way to develop empowering beliefs. When I started practicing simple living and eliminating physical clutter from my life, I was surprised by its magical effect.

Your life can be transformed when you start letting go of anything that is no longer useful. As you practice letting go of the unnecessary, you will develop the skill of letting go of limiting beliefs too.

When you create more space in your life for what matters most, you will extend this space to mental and emotional clutter as well.

Simple living is a great way to break free from anything that is pulling you down. You can check out my blog MidwaySimplicity.com for free articles and videos on how to simplify your life and enjoy more with less.

6. Try New Experiences

Practice a new skill, travel to a new place, experience different cultures, and get out of your comfort zone. Since your limiting beliefs were formed as a result of your life experiences, you can form new beliefs or let go of old ones by exposing yourself to new experiences. Overcoming limiting beliefs requires trying new experiences that challenge these beliefs or form new empowering ones.

By regularly stretching your mind and enriching your life with new experiences, you will challenge the strongest beliefs that might be holding you back from achieving what you want to do in life.

Trying new experiences gives you new eyeglasses through which you can see the world in a better and more informed way. It increases your possibilities and the person who has more possibilities usually wins (like my mentor Jim Cathcart used to say).

7. Keep a Journal

Keeping a journal is a great way to reflect on and examine your beliefs. When you put your thoughts on paper you gain more clarity and awareness of what is stoping you and what is empowering you.

When I started a gratitude journal I realized how much I was blessed. It made me realize that at any given moment in life, my blessings are much more than my problems.

Moreover, keeping an eye on what I was grateful for in my life attracted more of what I liked. It kind of activated the law of attraction!

I highly encourage you to start a gratitude journal today. And each day before you go to sleep write down one thing you were grateful for in that day. And begin to watch the magic!

You can choose to have empowering beliefs. Pick one of the seven ways above and start cultivating more empowering beliefs in your life. When your empowering beliefs become dominant, your life will turn into a life of success and significance. And you will become the heroic leader you want to be.

4. Rejecting Rejections

Heroic leaders reject rejections.

Let me share with you an inspiring story of an unusual pursuit of passion. It's a great model of how to achieve against the odds. Are you passionate about something unusual that has never been done before? Are you passionate about a certain idea that is contrary to the popular belief or trend?

If yes, then this story is for you.

He tried to kill himself twice at age 20 and 21. Forty years later, he considered himself to be one of the happiest people you'll ever know. He is known as the founding father of the International Firewalking Movement. He is the one who taught Tony Robbins how to firewalk!

He has resulted in a global phenomenon of over 3 million people attending Firewalking classes in six continents.

He is Tolly Burkan.

I was honored to interview Tolly a few years ago about his story of success and transformation.

Tolly was passionate about teaching people how to be happy. And when he discovered Firewalking (a practice that dated back to 1200 B.C.), he fell in love with the idea. He believed that it would be the ultimate vehicle through which he could help people transform their lives.

He believed that this was a cutting-edge method for developing human potential. He looked at Firewalking as a great metaphor that shows that personal power is gained through an inner state of heightened awareness and empowerment. If you can walk on fire, then what can you NOT do? The Firewalking experience melts down all the fears that may stop you from achieving your wildest dreams.

But, how on earth could he make a living out of it? In order to become successful, he needed to persuade people to walk barefoot over a bed of hot embers. How could someone build a profitable business around persuading people to walk on fire?

This was something that no one had done before. It was contrary to all popular beliefs and trends. And it was dangerous. Some people thought that what Tolly was doing was satanic — from the devil! So, he was up against public skepticism and religious criticism.

If you were there at the beginning of the Firewalking movement, you would think that this idea was destined to fail — guaranteed.

In his early days, Tolly burned a lot of people until he learned how to do this safely. At some point, he thought to himself that he shouldn't be doing this. But, if he had let his doubts stop him he wouldn't be where he is today. If he let other people's doubts stop him he wouldn't be THE founding father of Firewalking — a great life-transformation movement.

Look at Firewalking today.

Not only it is widely popular in the public circles, but it is being used by giant companies like Microsoft, American Express, Coca Cola, Met-Life and many more. They are all using it as a part of their training and empowerment programs.

How was all this possible?

Before, I share the secret with you, let me reveal another little-known fact about Tolly Burkan.

You might think that the public resistance to his crazy idea was enough of a challenge. But surprisingly, there was more.

Tolly had a physical disability.

In his 20's, a car ran through the red light,

hit him and threw him 25 ft. His neck was crushed, the whole left part of his body was paralyzed and he had too many surgeries. He never fully recovered from this accident. He has had five bones transplants in his neck alone and that's just a small example.

I want you to imagine how hard it is to deliver his Firewalking seminars and travel all over the world despite of this great physical challenge.

Was it easy? Absolutely not.

But, Tolly knew that most people are suffering because they don't know how to face their challenges, and therefore their challenges defeat them. He believed that his challenges were important, because without challenges he (and you) couldn't grow.

One of the things that helped him overcome his physical disability was that he found an inspiring role model who was totally paralyzed from neck down, yet he was a very successful author and professional speaker.

Now, back to the question of "How was all that possible?" What is the secret of his remarkable success?

Besides being extremely passionate, Tolly believed that the journey of a thousand miles begins with the first step and that sometimes this step might be contrary to the popular belief. That's why you must be patient, have a thick skin and persist.

In fact, in his first few years, things went very slowly. Doing something new that is contrary to the popular belief always faces a ton of resistance.

What motivated Tolly to persist is that he just focused more on the value he was giving to people and let the rest take care of itself. When he discovered and believed in the transformational impact and tremendous value of Firewalking, he stuck to the idea until he made it.

Follow the genuine inspiration that you feel in your heart, because that's what makes all the difference. They will think you're crazy, but you will know that this will bring you your ultimate dream.

Be receptive and stick to your unusual passionate ideas. Don't let the doubts stop you from following your passion and having a life you can be proud of.

Reject rejections and follow the genuine inspiration that comes from your heart. That's how you become a worldwide sensation and change the lives of millions.

Implementing the PERK system in your company requires a heroic leader. And you can easily become one, if you develop the above four traits: find direction in the darkness, reshape reality, cultivate empowering beliefs and reject rejections.

Expand your knowledge and experience so that you can find direction in the darkness.

Don't accept reality as it is. Always question and reshape reality.

Expose your mind to positive vibes in order to cultivate empowering beliefs.

And finally, reject rejections and stick to your revolutionary idea as long as you believe that it can add tremendous value to other people.

When you do that, you will be a heroic leader who can create a passion-driven culture where people feel great and at the same time maximize profits.

Now, let's recap...

9

WHAT IS YOUR PERK?

Let's summarize what we have been discussing so far.

The PERK system starts with bringing in passionate people who have infectious positive energy. Embrace or restore the passions of existing people. Passion goes around the company, and makes everyone love the work they are doing.

Then you inspire them with your story, and make them crazy about the company and its mission.

When they have maximized their energy, you need to channel it in ways that utilize their strengths and bring out the best in them. Focus on making their strengths even stronger.

Empower them by giving them the freedom and autonomy to work on tasks that make them feel strong, not tasks that drain their energy or make them feel weak.

Throughout the process, always monitor what stands between them and greatness. Act as a sweeper; remove anything that stands between them and becoming one of the great ones.

When they become the best they can be, show them more opportunities to rise and grow. Encourage them to share their hidden treasures, instead of being like the stainless guy.

Finally, provide them with world class training from experts by implementing and fully operating a training campaign that starts with marketing your programs as if they're going to pay for it from their salaries. Promise them that you are going to coach them to apply what they will learn – and do it. Ask them to come back with an action plan, and work with them to implement it inside the company so that you get value for the money you spent and effort you gave.

If you worry about investing in them only to have them leave, ask yourself about the risk of not investing in them, and what you may lose.

In the background of all that, work on making your company a place of a good karma, positive vibes and a great atmosphere that make a fun working environment and eliminate all the distractions and stress as much as possible. This will help boost their creativity and foster intense loyalty.

At the end, you may wonder, "This sounds like a great system. But, I'm just one man, -- or woman. I cannot change everything by my own."

That's why you need to develop the traits of heroic leadership. Heroes find a way in the darkness. Heroes reshape reality. Heroes use their empowering beliefs to find powerful breakthroughs. Heroes reject rejections and stick to their revolutionary idea.

Remember...

"One man with courage makes a majority."
- Andrew Jackson

One man with courage makes THE difference. I believe you have that courage inside you. You're THE hero we need in order to change the corporate culture and have more passion-driven companies.

You have the courage to make a difference, and act as a change and transformation catalyst inside your company. Since I believe that you have that courage, I will leave you with this question to think about.

As you finish reading this last paragraph, ask yourself:

"What will be my PERK (M&M candy)
for my people?"

Go to work tomorrow and do something different that surprises your people and shows that you are heading towards a new era of leading a passion-driven company.

You have that courage that makes a majority. You can make a difference, I believe in you.

Get ready to ...

PERK UP YOUR PROFITS

Best Regards,
Mohamed Tohami

ABOUT THE AUTHOR

Over the past nine years, Mohamed Tohami, bestselling author and Egypt's #1 motivation expert, has been helping thousands of people restore their passion for life and work.

He is on a mission to help individuals and organizations grow exponentially & maximize profits by unleashing the ultimate power of passion-driven work.

Tohami is known for his series of interviews with ultra-successful people about their secrets of success, and has recorded over 150 interviews with the world's leading success and business gurus including Jim Cathcart, Tony Alessandra, Michael Gerber, Mark Sanborn, and many more.

On May 19, 2009, his first book, The Pharaohs' Code, was Amazon's #1 best-selling motivational book. This book is your personal Rosetta Stone for unlocking the true meaning of your life. He is also the author of two internationally highly acclaimed books: *StoryNetworking: A Proven 4-Step System To Connect With Successful People* and *Midway Simplicity: Easy Solutions To Simplify Your Time, Health, Things, Finances and Relationships*.

He is the creator of the Passion To Profit Podcast, #1 business/career podcast on iTunes. It is the first motivational podcast in the Middle East that shows you how to find your passion and turn it into a profitable business.

Tohami lives in the land of the Pharaohs, Egypt, with his wife and little girl.

More about Tohami at:
www.tohami.com